# CHOOSING & US
# Flooring

# House Beautiful

# CHOOSING & USING

# Flooring

## Lucinda Richards

**Ebury Press**
London

First published 1995
1 3 5 7 9 10 8 6 4 2

This edition published in 1995 by
Ebury Press, Random House,
20 Vauxhall Bridge Road, London
SW1V 2SA

Random House Australia (Pty) Limited,
20 Alfred Street, Milsons Point,
Sydney,New South Wales 2061,
Australia

Random House New Zealand Limited
18 Poland Road, Glenfield,
Auckland 10, New Zealand

Random House South Africa (Pty)
Limited PO Box 337, Bergvlei,
South Africa

Random House UK Limited
Reg. No. 954009A

CIP catalogue record for this book is
available from the British Library.

ISBN 009 178981 8

Editor: Emma Callery
Designed by Jerry Goldie Graphic
Design London

Colour separations by HBM Print Ltd

Printed and bound in Singapore
by Tien Wah Press

# CONTENTS

# INTRODUCTION

Welcome to our *Choosing and Using* series of practical books. Every homeowner knows the problems that so often go with the pride in creating a comfortable and attractive place to live. So with this in mind, our clear guides have been created to form a useful and inspirational series to keep on hand while you choose and use the essential elements for every room. With *Flooring*, for example, we provide advice on anything from vinyl tiling to deep pile carpeting, and each section has their care and maintenance explained.

The other books in the series cover aspects in an equally detailed way and I know you'll find each book as useful and inspiring as every issue of *House Beautiful* magazine.

Pat Roberts Cairns
Editor

**Right** *The floor covering you choose will have an immediate impact on the overall look of a room so take care and time to make the right choice. This natural sisal floor covering has an interesting herringbone weave which complements its natural texture. It makes the perfect choice for this minimalist interior, toning with both walls and the chairs.*

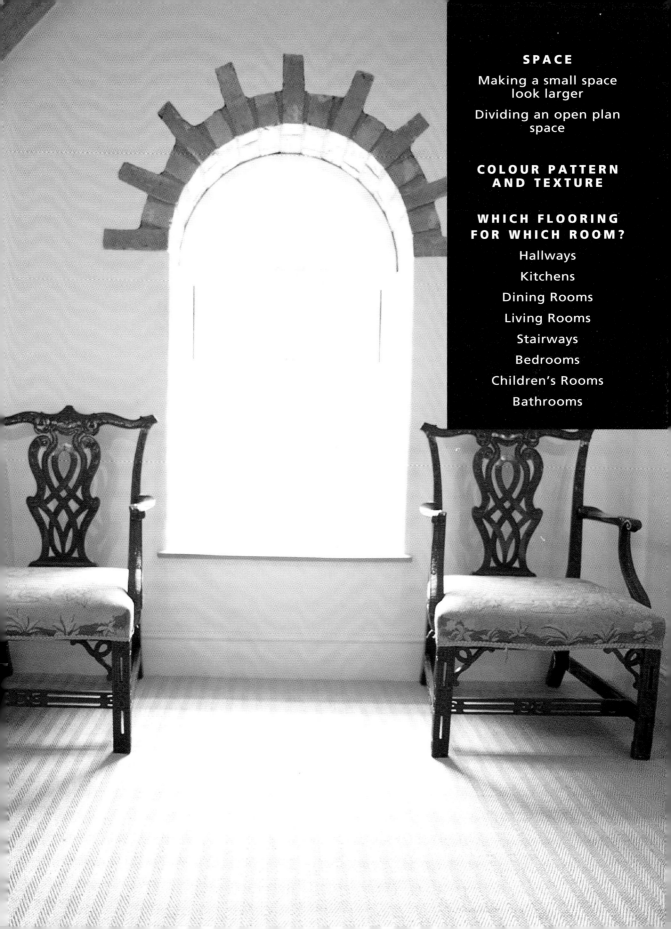

# SPACE

Used creatively, flooring can be one of the most effective means of defining space by linking or separating areas. In a large house with many rooms, different floorings can be used to increase the separate nature of each one: consideration must be given, however, to where the floorings meet. A highly patterned living room carpet leading on to another could look garish, so the overall scheme still has to be considered.

**Above** *When laying different floor coverings, make sure they don't clash. Here a flecked hallway carpet joins a plain living room carpet. Although they are different patterns and textures, tonally they are the same. As a result, they go well together but are dissimilar enough to maintain the separate nature of each room.*

## MAKING A SMALL SPACE LOOK LARGER

The same floor covering used throughout a small apartment will make it appear larger. Avoid the look becoming bland by introducing floorings of the same tone but of different textures. For example, sealed cork tiles in the kitchen, polished floorboards in the living areas and sisal in the hall all have a similar tonal quality but the textures are quite different. Such a scheme would also work well in a modern house where there are a number of rooms but space is at a premium.

## DIVIDING AN OPEN PLAN SPACE

Alternatively, you may wish to create divisions and different types of flooring can be used in open plan flats to define specific areas. For example, instead of using the same flooring throughout you could use rugs or kelims to define the sitting/socializing area, and vinyl or cork tiles for the kitchen area.

## BRIGHT IDEAS

❖ The same combination of tiles used in a variety of pattern can effectively separate off areas while maintaining the unity of the overall scheme.

❖ Stencilling on to floorboards or even cork titles is an attractive way of highlighting specific areas. For example, stencil a border around an eating area.

❖ Use other decorative paint effects (see pages 64-9) to define special areas: a cheap and effective way of creating instant 'rooms'.

*Left* *Using the same floor covering throughout a house to increase the feeling of space can become a little bland. Here floorings of the same tonal values but of different material and textures have been used to great effect. The quarry-tiled kitchen has its own natural patterning which meets effortlessly with the floorboards of the living area. A subtly patterned rug adds colour without detracting from the other floorings to create a classic country interior.*

# COLOUR, PATTERN AND TEXTURE

The colour, pattern or texture of a floor covering can dominate the way a room looks so take care to give it some careful consideration. Unless you are sure you want to make a definite statement, it is probably sensible to choose a floor covering that would suit other design schemes too.

## COLOUR

Consider the affect that different colours have on a room and how different colours work together. Pale colours, for example, create a greater feeling of space, whereas dark colours give a cosier, more intimate feel. A lot of research has been done into the psychological effects of colour and they may also be worth bearing in mind before you decide to paint your floor red and green. Blues are seen as soothing, calm colours; red is a stimulating one; greens are again relaxing, and yellows are energizing.

## PATTERN

Highly patterned floors, such as a chequerboard design or floral carpet, can be an immediate focal point. However, too many patterns can be difficult to cope with and means that any furnishings or wall coverings would have to be very plain.

Rugs are a good way of introducing pattern and colour to an area without the scheme dominating. Another more subtle form of patterning is the

*Above* Highly patterned floorings can be difficult to integrate with other furnishings, so unless you want them to dominate they are best avoided. More subtle patterns, such as those of this ethnic influenced carpet, are attractive options. The subtle terracotta tones of the background colour means it does not fight for attention while the strong but small areas of blue give vibrant colour interest.

*Left* This seagrass matting gives textural interest with its strong geometric design and colour combinations. It is unusual to find a flooring that can combine the three elements of colour, pattern and texture so successfully without dominating a room, but here it provides a natural foil to the dark wood of the furniture while the bold yellow stripes offset the neutral tones.

herringbone design of parquet flooring or the charmingly patterned and coloured inset tiles laid between terracotta or ceramic tiles.

## TEXTURE

Texture too is an important element of floorings and one that is becoming increasingly important in contemporary interiors as can be seen from the popularity of natural fabrics. Mattings such as sisal and coir all have distinctive textures which can be used to give interest throughout the house. Equally, the pile of a carpet, the grain of wood or contours of stone all give textural interest.

# WHICH FLOORING FOR WHICH ROOM?

You can lay whatever type of flooring you like in any room, but generally there are practical pointers that dictate what type would be most suitable for which room. For example, it is highly unlikely that you would want a cold stone floor in a bedroom, even if the sub-floor could take the weight. Equally, a pale-coloured carpet in a kitchen would obviously be impractical.

## HALLWAYS

Hallways probably get more wear than any other area of the house and were traditionally laid with stone flags or quarry tiles. Because of their hard wearing qualities and ease of cleaning these are still good choices, but unless you are fortunate enough to have one already in place it is an expensive option. There are other equally good, but slightly less expensive choices, however, such as wood, vinyl, coir or hard wearing carpet.

## KITCHENS

A hard flooring such as stone, slate, quarry or ceramic tiles would offer a practical solution for a kitchen area although if you often drop dishes then they will certainly break. They are also cold and hard to stand on so if you want something slightly softer, try vinyl, cork or lino tiles. You could also use carpet tiles but make sure they are suitable for kitchen use.

## DINING ROOMS

An ideal flooring for a dining room where accidents involving food and drink are likely to be a common occurrence is a wood floor which is easy to clean. Carpet is another possibility but would need regular cleaning and although

**Above** *Cushioned vinyl in a kitchen is an attractive and practical choice. This white chequerboard design with pale-grey insets harmonizes with the cool greys and whites of the fitted cupboards and furnishings, creating a calm, clean interior.*

ceramic tiles make an elegant choice, they are noisy and you would have to put up with the scraping of chairs. Natural mattings are not really suitable as food may get stuck between the fibres and make it impossible to clean. It is also worth remembering that a dining room may well double up as a work/study area so the flooring needs to be comfortable as well as practical.

**Above** *The flooring for a living room needs to be both hard wearing and visually appealing as we spend so much time in this area. Carpet is the natural choice for many people as it gives warmth and comfort. Make sure you choose the best you can afford: a wool or wool and nylon mix are both hard-wearing varieties.*

## LIVING ROOMS

In most modern households, the living room takes a huge amount of wear and tear but it also requires a flooring that looks good. Suitable soft floor coverings would include a wool or wool and nylon mix carpet, or a sisal or coir matting. Sanded down and sealed floorboards with colourful rugs would also be practical and attractive.

### STAIRWAYS

Again you need a hard wearing surface: a good quality carpet is ideal, as is natural seagrass (but not sisal as it becomes slippery with use). Long pile carpets should be avoided as the heel of a shoe could catch.

### BEDROOMS

Unlike most other areas you can let looks and comfort dominate your choice. Bedrooms are not generally heavy traffic areas and if you want a thick shag pile carpet then this is the room to have it in.

### CHILDREN'S ROOMS

In a child's room you really need a soft flooring which is also easy to maintain: vinyl or cork tiles are an ideal solution as both are hard wearing and easy to clean.

### BATHROOMS

Above all, bathroom floor coverings need to be waterproof: again vinyl makes an ideal choice. Ceramic tiles are popular but they can be extremely slippery when wet. Many people like carpet in a bathroom because it is soft and warm underfoot but while this is probably fine for a small household, a busy one may find it just gets too wet and begins to rot.

*__Right__ In a bedroom you can allow aesthetics to dominate over practicalities (unless it is a young child's room). This pretty checked rug laid over lime-washed boards creates a charming colonial style bedroom. It also matches the bedcovers and curtains perfectly while echoing the textures of the beautiful quilt hung on the wall.*

## PRACTICAL POINTERS

A new flooring can be an expensive outlay so it is worth asking yourself a few basic questions to narrow down the choices right from the start:

❖ Are you looking for a floor covering to use throughout the house or for a specific room?

❖ What activities will be carried out in the room?

❖ Does the floor covering need to be waterproof?

❖ Is the existing sub-floor in good condition?

❖ How much do you wish to spend?

❖ Are you likely to be moving in a few years time or do you literally want your floor covering to last a lifetime?

❖ Do you have young children?

❖ Is mud and dirt going to be bought into the room from outside?

❖ Do you like walking about the house barefoot?

Another factor that may narrow down your choice is if you want to do the job yourself. For example, laying cork, vinyl or carpet tiles is perfectly feasible for an amateur to carry out, but laying a stone floor or a fitted carpet is possible but not easy.

# CARPETS

Soft and warm underfoot, carpets more than any other type of floor-ing immediately give an interior a sense of luxury and comfort. They are, then, the first and immediate choice for many of us. A plain fitted carpet throughout a house gives a coordinated, spacious feel and works particulary well in interiors of limited space. It is in some respects a 'safe' choice but also a wise one as it can complement your curtains, walls and sofas in the best possible way. If you play too safe, however, the result can be rather bland and if this is your worry then remember there are a wonderful range of brightly-coloured rugs available that can introduce a splash of colour and pattern.

Highly patterned carpets have more often than not received rather a bad press and have long been associated with hotel and cin-ema lobbies along with piped music and plastic pot plants. This is a shame as there are some wonderful patterned carpets around that draw their inspiration from the designs of William Morris, Charles Voysey and Charles Rennie Mackintosh. They could be your ideal choice if you are trying to recreate a period feel in a Victorian or Edwardian property. They are also far more practical than plain car-pets as stains do not show.

*Right* This interestingly patterned carpet owes its influences to South American Inca traditions. It combines subtle colouring with intricate geometric patterns to create a harmonious and visually appealing flooring. The centrally placed rug effect gives an immediate focal point and breaks up the room into distinct areas. A patterned carpet such as this is a practical choice in a living area as marks will not show.

# CHOOSING CARPETS

There are a bewildering range of carpets available but the most important point to remember is that, in general, the more you pay, the better the quality. Although it may be tempting to go for a cheaper option it is a false economy and you'll probably end up paying more in the long run because a cheaper carpet will wear out more quickly and need to be replaced. Obviously, budgetary considerations are vital but go for the best you can afford. To make sure that you get value for money ensure you select the quality and style that is right for your lifestyle and home. Also bear in mind the durability and choice of colour.

*Below* This subtly flecked carpet is made from polypropylene, a hard-wearing, man-made fibre which is stain resistant making it an ideal choice for a hall or stairway carpet. Such carpets are also extremely good value.

*Right* The luxury of wool combined with the hard-wearing qualities of nylon make a wool/nylon mix carpet the best choice for a living room carpet. This contemporary design finds its inspiration from traditional kelims of North Africa and here makes the ideal partner to rattan furniture.

When buying a carpet take a sample of the carpet home with you so that you can see it under natural and artificial light and check that it goes with your existing furnishings. Always get a professional to measure up as mistakes can be costly. Check too that the price you have been quoted by the carpet showroom includes underlay and fixing materials such as gripper rods. You may find that what seems like an absolute bargain in one shop may, in fact, work out to be more expensive because of all the hidden extras.

## QUALITY

Unfortunately there is no one standard grading scheme common to all carpets. Individual manufacturers and retailers have their own systems so always check the labels which should provide all the information you need. Some use a numbering system which is simple and straightforward:

1 Very heavy wear (high quality for commercial use).
2 Heavy wear (living rooms, halls, stairs and landings).
3 Medium wear (dining rooms).
4 Light wear (bedrooms and bathrooms).
5 Luxury (longer-pile carpets, which are not necessarily very hard-wearing).

The pile weights per sq m (yd), usually given on the labels, are a very good guide to go by. For example, the minimum quality for a living room carpet used by two adults should be about 875g (31oz) per sq m (yd). For a family of four, where the wear will be greater, it should be 925 or 950g (33 or 34oz) per sq m (yd).

For halls, stairs and landings the minimum pile weight for family use should be 1kg (35oz) per sq m (yd). For bedrooms and lesser-used rooms, lighter weights - under 800g (28oz) - are usually suitable.

Originally, carpets were made from wool and top quality carpets still are made from a 100 per cent wool. Generally, however, the best mixture is 80/20 wool to nylon, which combines the resilience of the natural wool with the strength and toughness of man-made nylon. As the percentage of wool decreases so does the quality. However, man-made fibres are now much better than they use to be and modern technology has largely counteracted the old problems of static, staining and inflammability, so there is no longer a wide gulf between man-made and wool fibres in carpets.

# MAKING YOUR CHOICE

Carpets are constructed in different ways. Some are woven, others tufted. But while it is worth knowing about the types that are available, the durability and quality of the carpet is dictated more by the materials the carpet is made from than its construction.

## WHAT'S WHAT

### Axminster carpets

These are woven on traditional looms, which put the tufts into position and cuts them into a pile at the same time. This type of carpet is named after the company who first made them, although nowadays they are made by many different manufacturers. They are usually patterned with up to as many as 36 colours in any one design. They are fairly expensive carpets in the medium- to high-quality range.

### Wilton carpets

These carpets are also called after their original manufacturer and are again woven. Unlike Axminster carpets, however, they are usually plain or have no more than about five colours in a small pat-

*Left* The smooth pile of this plain velour carpet creates a clean uncluttered feel which can help to expand a small interior. The blue of the carpet is picked up and echoed in the curtains, cushions and sofa while the yellow walls provide the necessary contrast.

tern. They either have a cut or a loop pile - also known as Brussels weave (see below). The pile fibre, usually wool, is woven into the actual backing of the carpet (you can see it if you turn the carpet over), making it more expensive and generally of a higher quality than Axminsters.

### Brussels weave carpets

Also known as loop pile, the pile of these carpets is literally made up of a series of loops. They are hard wearing and tend to be at the more expensive end of the market.

### Tufted carpets

These are generally cheaper than woven ones as the fibres are rapidly inserted into the backing with dozens of sewing-machine-type needles. The pile is then secured with adhesive and a secondary backing added to give more strength.

### Cut and loop pile carpets

As the name suggests, these carpets are made with a combination of cut and looped pile, which creates a sculpted look. This type of carpet usually comes in plain colours only.

### Cut pile carpets

These are made up of single upright tufts. The term applies to a number of carpet types - Saxony, Hard twist and velvet (see below).

### Saxony carpets

Traditionally these were long-pile carpets suitable for low-traffic areas such as bedrooms. Shorter-pile Saxony weave carpets are more common these days

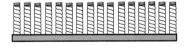

and although harder wearing they are still most suited to low-traffic areas.

### Hard twist carpets

Here the yarn is slightly twisted to create a hard-wearing carpet. Its tight texture means that foot marks don't show.

### Velvet or velour carpets

These have a very smooth pile which is extrasoft underfoot and yet fairly hard-wearing. Its smooth surface, however, means that foot marks tend to show.

### Carpet tiles

You can also buy carpets in tile form, which are easy to lay yourself (see page 46). They come in a range of sizes, patterns and colours, so you can create different effects whether it's a chequerboard, plain or a bordered style carpet you want. They are a practical option for children's rooms or dining rooms as any tiles which become particularly dirty or

damaged can be removed and replaced with a new one. Backed with rubber, they can be loose laid or stuck down. Some manufacturers even produce carpet tiles that are suitable for kitchens. Be careful how you use them, however. As they are so practical, they often find their way into commercial and public buildings which means they can give a room a work-like feel.

**Right** Carpet tiles are an interesting alternative to fitted carpets and have the advantage that they can be laid by the amateur.

*Above* A fitted carpet is normally seen as a traditional and safe choice for a floor covering. But there are also many exciting contemporary designs which add a touch of style and humour to an interior, such as this fake rug effect carpet. Its bold stripes and grids are a welcome change from the more normal florals.

## UNDERLAY

A good underlay will ensure your carpet lasts longer and make it more comfortable to walk on as it acts as a shock absorber between the carpet and floor. Some carpets come with an inbuilt foam backing and won't need underlay but it is advisable to at least lay them on paper to stop dust penetration and to prevent the foam backing from sticking to the floor.

## WHAT'S WHAT

*Felt underlays* These are made from compressed fibres, usually wool, left over from carpet pile, and are therefore very soft and springy. They make the best choice of underlay for quality woven carpets such as Wiltons and Axminsters.

*Rubber underlays* These are best used with tufted carpets.

# USING CARPETS
## Moving a stair carpet

Laying a fitted carpet is not easy and is really something that is best left to professional carpet fitters. If you buy your carpet through a reputable dealer they will give you a quote for fitting or recommend someone to do the job. If not, the National Institute of Carpet Fitters (see page 77) will give you the names of qualified fitters in your area.
A useful DIY job that can be done by the amateur, however, is to re-lay a stair carpet. This is worth doing once it shows signs of wear as it really prolongs the life of the carpet because it will wear more evenly. Use one-piece carpet grippers, available in three lengths.

### WHAT TO DO

**YOU WILL NEED**

One-piece carpet grippers

Nails

Hammer

Fitting tool (optional)

Carpet tacks

**BRIGHT IDEAS**

❖ Use carpet tiles to create patterned floorings.

❖ When initially laying a stair carpet, ensure that you have surplus carpet left at the top and bottom to allow for future re-lays.

❖ You could encourage family members to try to vary their route up the stairs, so that they don't always walk up the middle!

**1** Take up the carpet.

**2** Nail the carpet grippers into the angle between the tread and riser of each step.

**3** Starting at the top, move the carpet up or down by about 7.5cm (3in) from its old

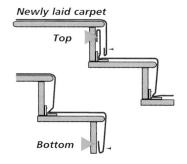

*Newly laid carpet*

Top

Bottom

position, according to where you have the most surplus, and tack it into place on the riser.

**4** A fitting tool can be hired to help you press the carpet firmly on to the gripper points. Pull the carpet taut over the step, down the riser and on to the next gripper pins, until you reach the bottom.

**5** Turn in the surplus at the bottom and tack it under. The carpet can be lifted and laid again whenever necessary.

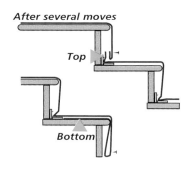

*After several moves*

Top

Bottom

# Care and maintenance

❖ You can vacuum a newly-laid carpet although avoid doing so excessively. If the carpet is shedding a lot of fluff you may find it easier to brush this up before vacuuming. Carpets need to be kept free of dirt as once dirt particles become trapped in the fibres they begin to cut through them. Regular vacuuming is therefore the best care you can give a carpet - at least once a week, and more often in busy areas of the home. If you have a long-pile carpet then this will benefit from an occasional comb with a special lightweight carpet rake.

❖ Furniture tends to leave marks on carpets, so if you like moving your furniture around then it is best to put furniture cups under particulary heavy pieces. Wool carpets are very forgiving and generally spring back into shape but even so you would be advised to use cups if you wish to avoid indentations.

**Left** *The life of a stair carpet, which receives a huge amount of wear and tear, can be prolonged by re-laying it to ensure a more even wear.*

## REMOVING STAINS

Unfortunately, spillages are a part of everyday life, especially if you have children. Mop up any liquid spills as quickly as possible - don't leave them. Kitchen or any other absorbent paper is the best thing to use to mop up the liquid. If you need to, use a little washing-up liquid or carpet shampoo and work from the outside of the stain inwards and don't rub too hard. Once it has dried, vacuum the area. Take care never to over wet a carpet as this may distort the backing fabric.

Many carpets now come with a protective finish which helps prevent staining and makes them easier to clean. Do not expect miracles, however - spillages still need to be cleaned up immediately and protective surfaces do not last forever. However, you can always have your carpet treated again to maintain its resistance.

## CLEANING

Shampooing carpets need only be done about once a year if they are vacuumed regularly. You can either do this your-self using a reputable brand of neutral dry foam shampoo or get a professional firm of cleaners to do it for you. If you decide on the DIY route, make sure you follow the instructions carefully and vacuum the carpet thoroughly before shampooing. Do not over wet the carpet as this can distort the underlay and make it difficult for the carpet to dry out. In extreme cases, it may even begin to rot.

**Right** Black is not normally an immediate colour choice for a carpet, not least because it would show marks. But this smartly striped black carpet breaks all the rules and would make a good choice for a teenager's bedroom. It is constructed from man-made stain resistant fibres and is bleach cleanable.

### PRACTICAL POINTERS

❖ Vacuum carpets at least once a week.

❖ Use furniture cups under particularly heavy pieces.

❖ Always blot up liquids rather than rubbing them into the carpet.

❖ Never over wet the area that you are cleaning.

❖ Always follow cleaning preparation instructions.

## STAIN REMOVAL GUIDE

Accidents are bound to happen but if you act quickly you should be able to prevent staining. You will need some clean absorbent tissue or kitchen roll to blot up any liquids and the following four basic solutions:

**1** Detergent solution made from 5ml (1 tsp) of gentle detergent (the type suitable for washing woollens) to 250ml ($\frac{1}{2}$ pint) of warm water.

**2** Bleach solution made by adding 15ml (1 tbsp) of household bleach to 1 cup of warm water.

**3** Dry cleaning solvent.

**4** Detergent and vinegar solution made by adding 5ml (1 tsp) of white wine (not malt) vinegar to the detergent solution.

| Stain | Action |
|---|---|
| *Alcohol, tea, coffee and urine* | Blot up the liquid with absorbent tissue or cloths. Wash with a little of the detergent solution. Work from the outer edge of the stain inwards. |
| *Chocolate, sweets, blood, glue, egg, ice-cream, milk and vomit* | Scrape up any excess with a blunt knife Wash with the detergent solution, working from the outside inwards. Blot dry and then apply a little of the bleach solution. Blot dry. |
| *Fats, tar, chewing gum, oil, ointments and shoe polish* | Scrape up any excess with a blunt knife. Use the dry cleaning solvent followed by the detergent and vinegar solution. Blot dry. |

# NATURAL FLOOR COVERINGS

Carpets made from natural materials such as jute, seagrass, rushes and coir have been around for centuries. The ancient Egyptians used bulrushes to weave mats and in medieval England loose rushes and reeds were strewn over floors.

More recently, coir and sisal were favoured for their hard wearing properties and cheapness but still viewed as the paupers of the carpet world. Recently, however, the vogue for neutral earth tones and natural products has ensured their passage from National Trust properties and student bedsits to the homes of the chic and stylish. In essence, natural floor coverings suit any household and are a viable alternative to carpets - even for bedrooms.

Available in a wide range of colours and weaves from a dark honey bouclé to a midnight-blue Jacquard, whatever your colour preferences, there is plenty of choice. Some ranges are also much softer underfoot than the original seagrass and coir mattings, so don't dismiss them from bedrooms.

The natural textures give added interest to any interior and they work well with brightly-coloured rugs or throws for a slightly ethnic look, or used throughout an open-plan flat they give a stylish and elegant continuity. Their universal appeal means they are equally at home in either a contemporary or period home.

*Right The soft textures and subtle colour tones of natural mattings provide an easy and workable backdrop to any interior. They go particularly well with today's simpler interiors. Here, seagrass matting provides the ideal link between indoors and outdoors.*

**CHOOSING WHAT
YOU NEED:**

What's what

**USING NATURAL
FLOOR
COVERINGS:**

Binding matting

Care and
maintenance

Laying

# CHOOSING NATURAL FLOOR COVERINGS

There are now a number of companies specializing in natural floor coverings and a wide variety of materials are used. Whereas natural floor coverings traditionally meant coir or seagrass you can now buy sisal, jute or rush mattings too.

The properties of the different materials vary, and some, such as jute, have slightly softer textures which means they are suitable for bedrooms. They are not, however, as hard wearing as the others so aren't really suitable for through ways. Generally, natural mattings don't make a great choice for bathrooms where excessive moisture may make them warp and drag. Also, in kitchens and dining rooms crumbs and dirt may gather in the weave.

One of their main advantages, however, is that they blend beautifully with almost any furnishing scheme - period or contemporary - which makes them the ideal backdrop for other materials.

Colours are usually beiges, browns or gold, although some natural fibres can be dyed in other colours, or have different fibres mixed in to create a variety of patterns and textures.

**Left** *This jute rug provides a natural partner to the polished floorboards. Neither are competing for attention, but when combined they create a harmonious and relaxing interior.*

## WHAT'S WHAT

**Coir** This is made from the thick, prickly fibre which comes from coconuts (a less refined version is used to make doormats). Available in a variety of colours, thicknesses and weaves, it's the ideal low-cost flooring solution for hallways and stairs. It can also be bought as square tiles with a strong rubber backing.

**Seagrass** So-called because it is grown in paddy-like fields and given a flooding of sea-water during the crop cycle, seagrass is extremely hard wearing. It has an almost impermeable fibre which is naturally stain resistant and also dye resistant. This means it cannot satisfactorily be dyed and so comes in its natural colours - a random mix of beige and yellow with hints of russet and green.

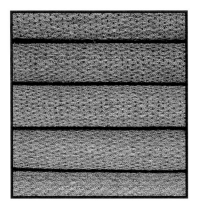

**Sisal** This matting comes from the dark green spiky leaves of the *Agave sisalana* bush which is grown in sub-tropical climates. It is soft enough for bedrooms and tough enough for stairs. Sisal is available in a number of weaves, including herringbone, twill, plain, and a variety of different colour combinations.

**Jute** Made from the jute plant, the stalks are softened in water like coir husks, and the fibre is then stripped

**Left** *Seagrass is naturally stain resistant so it cannot be dyed. But by introducing different colour wefts a delightful range of subtle patterns and colour schemes can be achieved.*

**Below** *If you want a different pattern or colour to that normally associated with natural mattings, then sisal comes in colours ranging from deep red to midnight blue plus some subtler colour variations.*

away. Not quite as hard-wearing as sisal, it is also rather softer and makes an ideal floor covering for bedrooms. It is available in its natural colour, bleached or dyed, and in a number of different weaves.

**Rush** Made from hand-plaited strips of rush, this type of flooring can be used both as a fitted covering or as loose laid mats. As rushes do not like to become too dry, this matting works very well in conservatories and is perfectly happy on floors which are not totally damp-proof (provided that there is adequate ventilation).

### PRACTICAL POINTERS

❖ As a general rule, the more hard-wearing varieties make an ideal choice for heavy traffic areas such as hallways, stairs (follow the manufacturer's laying instructions carefully), and living rooms.

❖ Natural floor coverings are available as separate squares, some with rubber backs for extra strength and practicality, as fitted lengths or as mats and runners.

❖ Runners are particularly good for taking the chill off a stone flagged hall or in a conservatory to give warmth.

❖ You can also take runners with you when you move house.

# USING NATURAL FLOOR COVERINGS

## Binding matting

Sisal, cord and coconut matting will fray at the edges unless they have a satisfactory latex border on both sides of the matting. You can bind any small rug or carpet this way but ensure it is completely clean, or the adhesive won't stick.

### WHAT TO DO

**1** Trim the edges with the knife or sharp scissors.

**2** Cut the binding tape to the required length and

squeeze or paint the latex adhesive along half the width of the tape. Glue the same width along one edge of the matting. When nearly dry, stick the two coated sides together.

**3** Turn the matting over and repeat the process with the other half of the tape.

**4** Tap along both sides with the hammer to make sure the tape and matting bond together.

## Care and maintenance

Natural floor coverings are very forgiving and hard wearing but even such resilient materials benefit from a little care and attention and by taking a few simple precautions you can ensure you get the most out of your flooring.

❖ Some natural mattings come with a latex backing and these are the easiest to keep clean as the backing prevents any build-up of grime beneath. Simply vacuum it regularly, to keep the dust levels to a minimum.

❖ Unbacked varieties will allow a lot of dust through, and the flooring will have to be rolled back from time to time so that the surface beneath can be cleaned.

❖ Lift furniture over it, without dragging, to avoid rucking and splitting the weave.

❖ Staining on some of the light-coloured varieties can be a problem but damage can be limited by prompt action after a spillage. If staining does occur then you can buy a special proprietary treatment for natural fibres.

❖ To ensure the matting stays neat, cut off any loose, split or jagged ends that appear.

## LAYING

Underlay is not absolutely necessary for natural mattings but if your floor is particularly uneven it is probably advisable to use one. Latex-backed varieties should be stuck directly to the floor with double-sided tape. Or use a special carpet glue that does not leave a sticky residue on the existing floor if you decide to take up the natural matting.

Matting that comes in squares can be loose laid by stitching the squares together using twine. This is a DIY job but matting laid in this way probably won't last as long as those installed by a professional fitter who will stretch the matting correctly as it is laid.

If you do decide to lay your own matting then make sure you cut it slightly bigger than required and allow it to stand in the room where it is to be laid for 24 hours as it will dry out slightly and contract.

❖ Natural matting, especially rush, will benefit from an occasional watering. Some manufacturers provide a special watering can when you buy your matting but otherwise a normal watering can will do. Make sure you don't over wet it, however, as it will rot.

*Above* One of the great advantages of natural mattings is that they are extremely hard wearing and almost maintenance free. Simply vacuum clean, cut off any loose ends that appear and then 'water' rush matting, and it will go on and on.

### BRIGHT IDEAS

❖ Bind small offcuts to make placemats.

❖ Make a small mat as a covering for a tiled kitchen or hall floor by stitching together leftover squares of seagrass for example, or simply bind the edges of leftover lengths.

# RUGS

Rugs come in all shapes, sizes and textures from exquisitely woven Chinese or Persian rugs to the more homely handmade braided, rag or hooked rugs. Originally they were considered too precious to place on the floor and were used to drape over furniture and tables or hung on walls. Nowadays we have access to rugs from all over the world and so can choose from an enormous range of colours, styles and price ranges.

One of the most glorious aspects of rugs is their movability - you can try them out all over the house where they will give instant colour and pattern to any scheme. And if you become bored with the look you can easily change it. Ideal for giving added warmth to hard flooring such as slate, marble or stone, they can also be used to create a rich, layered look over plain fitted carpets. Rugs are particularly useful for protecting carpets in areas where they are likely to get much wear such as in front of the sofa, fireplace or inside a hallway. There are also some delightful animal and alphabet designs which are ideal for children's rooms. They are cheap and machine washable.

Whatever your choice, enjoy their versatility: drape an Indian dhurry over a sofa or table for an interesting ethnic look, or display an Oriental carpet on a wall for a more exotic feel.

**Right** Used imaginatively and creatively, rugs can turn an ordinary interior into a cornucopia of colour, pattern and texture. This exquisite tribal rug was made using coarse handspun wool coloured with bright vegetable dyes. The simple images of birds and animals against the blue ground have created a rug that would look at home in a country interior or a city apartment.

**CHOOSING WHAT YOU NEED:**
What's what

**USING RUGS:**
Making a rag rug
Care and maintenance

# CHOOSING RUGS

Your choice will be dictated by price and for which room you want the rugs. Generally, rugs come in all shapes and sizes, from cheap and cheerful, machine-washable ones ideal for nurseries, to woven or luxury hand-tufted varieties. In between there is a wealth of rag rugs, dhurries and flat-woven rugs. These can be soft and tactile, or tough and hard-wearing if made from materials such as coir, rush or jute.

*(Above) There are many cheap rugs available that make ideal coverings for children's rooms as they can easily be washed. Usually made of cotton or chenille, such rugs are a cheap and cheerful way of brightening up a room.*

**Bokhara rugs** A fine cut-pile wool rug from Pakistan, hand-washed to give a very high sheen.

**Chinese rugs** Made from wool or silk, Chinese rugs have a thick rich feel with textured surfaces made by carving out designs with hand-held electric scissors. The softness and variation in colour attained by the Chinese is enhanced by the washing process which adds shine and lustre to the final rug.

**Dhurries (or dhurrys)** Indian flat-woven rugs, which are usually made from cotton although some more expensive types may contain wool or silk. They come in a wide range of colours from pale pastels to bright primaries and because they are the same on both sides they can be reversed. Their generally bold geometric designs give them a young contemporary feel. Some dhurries can be quite cheap, others fairly expensive.

**Kelims** These are flat-woven wool carpets from Turkey or Afghanistan. They are tapestry woven which means they have no pile and generally have geometric patterns. Kelims are often used as wall hangings. They can be quite expensive.

**Numdahs** Embroidered rugs from Kashmir, made from wool and cotton, felted together under water pressure.

**Persian rugs** Here is the archetypal magic carpet of Aladdin and many other children's stories. Originally from central Asia, there are now many different sorts of Persian rugs, some made in India and others even made in Britain. Knotted in wool (or silk) on to a woven base, traditional colours were reds and blues. Good Persian carpets can be extremely expensive.

*There are a huge variety of rugs available from the simple, patterned ethnic kelims and dhurries (**above and below**) to the more sophisticated patterns of the archetypal magic Persian carpets (**opposite**). The latter are particulary soft underfoot and its use here beside a bed is an ideal choice - what could be more luxurious than stepping out on to the soft thick pile of a Persian rug?*

**Rag, braided or hooked rugs** Originally from Sweden, where they were made from strips of old clothing, the modern versions are flat-woven cotton and come in a choice of neutral or cheerful colours. A word of warning, it is not advisable to lay rag rugs on top of pale-coloured carpets.

## PRACTICAL POINTERS

❖ A good-quality rug should be dense and firm, whether flat-woven or fibre pile.

❖ Most pile rugs are 100 per cent pure new wool: the Woolmark symbol is an assurance that it meets specified standards. Cotton, jute and sometimes linen are also used.

❖ Be sure it is well finished, with no ragged edges.

❖ Always buy from a reputable retailer.

# USING RUGS
## Making a rag rug

A rag rug is ideal for using leftover pieces of fabric although make sure they are of similar weights and that you have a lot of them as it takes a surprising amount to make a rug.

## WHAT TO DO

**1** Using an iron, press in the raw edges of the fabric lengthwise to make a 6mm ($1/4$ in) hem on each side. Then press the strip in half length-wise so the raw edges do not show. You need to prepare plenty of strips in this way.

**2** Take three fabric strips and stitch the ends together. Then plait the fabric together making sure that you keep an even tension. When you run out of fabric, simply stitch another strip on to the end.

**3** Keep plaiting until you have a plait several metres long. Then begin to coil the plait around, and slip stitch in place to form a rug. Stitch the loose ends of the end of the plait into the back of the rug to finish it off neatly.

*Left* Don't just look upon rugs as floor coverings. They can be hung from the wall or draped over sofas, chairs and tables to create instant areas of interest. These wonderful kelims give this modern interior an ethnic look that works well with the terracotta tones of the tiled floor.

## Care and maintenance

❖ Vacuum regularly, as you would a carpet. For longer-pile rugs, use either a suction cleaner or an upright one which has been adjusted to a suitable height so that the pile will not become entangled.

❖ Before cleaning, always check for any instructions on the label. Some rugs are marked machine-wash or hand-wash; others should be dry-cleaned. As with fitted carpets deal with spillages as they occur (see Stain Removal Guide, page 27).

❖ To even out wear and fading, move rugs around regularly.

❖ Rugs can be hazardous, especially if loose laid on polished wooden floors. To prevent accidents it is a good idea to secure them with some sort of underlay. There are a variety of anti-slip materials available for use with rugs and such an underlay would also prevent colours from non-dye-fast rugs staining a fitted carpet.

# TILES

Now available in a huge range of materials, colours, textures and sizes, tiles can be the ideal flooring solution not just for kitchens and bathrooms but for other areas of the house too. If they are well-laid and used imaginatively, tiles can give a room a distinctive and stylish finish that is also practical. A patterned tiled floor will immediately become a focal point, for example, so care should be taken that you choose an appropriate design and colour that suits your style. For example, black and white for a kitchen, or blue and white for a bathroom are both classic colour schemes that won't date. Large slate or stone flags in a hall or living area give a grand, classic look but would probably only suit a larger scale house while smaller tiles would look good in a smaller room.

If you want a Mediterranean feel try cool white tiles or for a country look warm-toned quarry tiles. Cork, vinyl or lino tiles give a warmth underfoot that is often practical for colder climates while offering a stunning variety of styles and colours. Polished cork for a child's bedroom is both practical and attractive while cushioned vinyl or lino for a kitchen or bathroom is a natural and practical choice.

**Right** Traditional quarry flags are the ideal choice for this country kitchen with its wooden beams and cupboards. Easy to clean and hard wearing, they make a practical solution for a hard-working area such as the kitchen.

**CHOOSING WHAT YOU NEED:**

Hard flooring

Soft flooring

What's what

**USING TILES:**

Laying soft tiles

Laying hard tiles

Care and maintenance

# CHOOSING TILES

Tiles break down into two distinctive types - hard and soft. Hard varieties include ceramic, quarry, marble, slate and stone while soft varieties include cork, lino and vinyl. As a general rule, hard varieties tend to be more expensive - although some types of lino and vinyl can be costly too - and more difficult to lay yourself. Before deciding which flooring is most suitable, always take into account the kind of wear it will get and what you expect from it.

## Hard versus soft flooring

❖ Warmth: will you be standing on the floor for long periods of time? Do members of your family like to walk about barefoot?
❖ Safety: if there are very young or elderly people in the house, avoid potentially slippery floorings or very hard ones.
❖ Noise: hard flooring tends to be noisy, while soft surfaces tend to absorb noise. For a quiet life, it's always worth insulating the sub-floor before laying the new floor on top.
❖ Installation: will the flooring need to be laid professionally? If so, bear this extra cost in mind when you are budgeting. If laying it yourself, make sure you follow the instructions exactly.

### HARD FLOORING

All types of hard flooring will literally last for a lifetime, so buy them as a long-term investment. Easy to clean and extremely hard-wearing, they are ideal for any room that is subject to the constant heavy traffic of a busy family. The main drawback, however, is that all hard floors are cold and unyielding underfoot, so they can be tiring to stand on for long periods. And although they are practical for kitchens, any dropped dishes will certainly break.

Waterproof and easy to clean, hard flooring is also ideal for bathrooms, with soft rugs providing the necessary warmth. From an aesthetic point of view, the subtle colours and textures of natural stones would enhance any interior.

*Below* The natural textures and colouring of these slate tiles create their own random patterns and harmonize well with the wooden fitted cupboards. Extremely hard wearing, a floor such as this will last forever.

❖ Hard flooring is expensive so don't make costly mistakes. Count part tiles as whole tiles for estimating purposes (see page 46) but remember that one tile can be cut into several border pieces.

❖ Always allow a few extra tiles - about 5 per cent - for breakages and future repairs. Check tiles for chips and colour differences. You may have to mix boxes for a random colour distribution.

❖ Hard floor tiles are heavy and difficult to cut and although you can hire a special tile-cutter, you may prefer to leave the job to a professional. All hard flooring needs a strong, perfectly flat sub-floor, so if the existing floorboards are very uneven it may be better to take them up and replace the boards with 12mm (1/2in) exterior-grade chipboard screwed into the joists. Alternatively, sheets of 12mm (1/2in) plywood could be screwed directly onto the existing boards. Hardboard would not be rigid enough to ensure a totally flat surface.

❖ Ceramic tiles must be laid with special tiling adhesive (all other hard floorings are laid in a bed of mortar cement).

❖ You have to be careful that the sub-floor can take the weight of your flooring as marble, slate and stone can be extremely heavy once laid.

## SOFT FLOORING

Although not as hard wearing as the hard varieties, soft floorings are generally less expensive and if you are keen on DIY, they are easier to lay than hard tiles. Cork tiles, in particular, are cheap and can be laid by an absolute beginner. They also make much safer surfaces for young children to play on. The other joy about soft floorings is that they come in such a variety of colours and patterns that you can imitate almost any other sort of flooring.

*Above* This attractive vinyl flooring imitates that of a natural terracotta tiled floor with striking white and blue diamond inserts.

# MAKING YOUR CHOICE

The choice of tiles is wide and you can really only make it once you have made the initial decision of looking for a hard or soft flooring. HF = hard flooring  SF = soft flooring

## WHAT'S WHAT

### Ceramic tiles (HF)

Made of clay by hand or by machine and fired at a high temperature, they can be glazed or unglazed and are thicker than wall tiles. They come in an enormous range of patterns, sizes and shapes from French Provençal pammets to traditional Victorian style tiles so you are sure to find something to suit your needs. Vitrified ceramic tiles are frost-proof so could be used in conservatories and on patios and swimming pool surrounds but they would not be able to stand up to severe weather conditions.

Impervious to most household liquids, ceramic tiles are easy to clean but can be noisy, cold and tiring to stand on. They can also be very slippery when wet.

### Quarry tiles (HF)

These are unglazed ceramic tiles, available in a range of natural colours from yellow, through shades of red to brown. They have a very slightly softer surface than ceramic tiles and after years of use may begin to wear slightly giving them an authentic country look. In

fact, some manufacturers will supply you with 'antique' terracotta and quarry tiles which have been taken from their original site and cleaned for re-use. Again they are hard underfoot but easy to keep clean.

### Marble tiles (HF) A

hard-wearing natural stone which is available in large, thick slabs and as thin-cut tiles. It must be laid in a

**Above** Tiles are often confined to kitchens and bathrooms but these old quarry tiles make a wonderful flooring for this period living room. They tone very well with the decor and furnishings and the throws provide a splash of colour and warmth underfoot.

cement bed, on a strong concrete sub-floor. Good for creating stunning floors but it is very expensive and also stains quite easily (See Care and Maintenance on page 49).

**Slate tiles** (HF) Slate is another hard-wearing natural stone that comes in a range of subtle soft colours, all with a rippled, layered-look, non-slip finish (see also page 72).

**Stone slabs** (HF) Limestone and granite floors come in large slabs looking more like paving stones than tiles. Both are extremely hard-wearing but look most effective when laid in more simple, country-style settings. They are also suitable for outdoor use (see also page 72).

**Cork tiles** (SF) Cork comes as tiles or less commonly in 'planks'. Made from cork granules with natural or synthetic binders, cork is a natural insulator and the ideal choice for a chilly kitchen or bathroom floor. It is also a practical choice for children's bedrooms. It comes unsealed - the cheapest option - or sealed with a clear vinyl layer. Sealed or unsealed, it is very good value especially as it is so easy to lay yourself (see overleaf).

**Linoleum** (SF) Commonly called lino, this is made from a mixture of ground cork, wood, flour, linseed oil and resins, all pressed on to a jute or hessian backing. It went out of fashion for 20 years or so when vinyl was first introduced but now this extremely durable flooring is rightly making a comeback. No other product can boast that it actually gets tougher with age. The secret lies with the linseed oil which continues to mature for at least ten years after manufacture. Available in different grades and thicknesses, lino comes both as a sheet material and in pre-cut tiles, which you can make into the most stunning range of patterns. You can also commission special designs, which is obviously expensive, but ensures you have a unique floor.

**Vinyl** (SF) There are several types of vinyl available and like lino it is available in sheet or tile form. All vinyl is waterproof and resistant to oil, grease and most household chemicals making it an ideal choice for kitchens and bathrooms. It is also non-allergenic, which for some households could make life easier. It comes in several different grades to suit various rooms.

Standard vinyl is flexible but thin, cold to walk on and can be hard underfoot. However, on the plus side it is cheap. Cushioned vinyl is made up rather like a sandwich with a spongy layer between the top and the backing, making it a soft, quiet and comfortable floor

**Above** These fresh green and white ceramic floor tiles are an ideal choice for a conservatory where you need a surface that is going to be hard wearing and waterproof.

covering to walk on but also making it more expensive than standard vinyl. Use 1.5mm ($^1/_{16}$in) thicknesses for bathrooms and bedrooms and up to 3.5mm ($^1/_8$in) for kitchens and halls.

Vinyl comes in a vast range of patterns and textures and some is made to imitate other floorings such as wood, marble, tiles and stones, and can create beautifully realistic finishes. You can also mix colours and patterns to create unique effects, especially with some of the border designs.

Vinyl tiles always come in packs, so check that the code number is the same on each one otherwise the colour may not match.

# USING TILES
## Laying soft tiles

It is possible to lay cork, vinyl and lino flooring yourself in tile form although the sub-floor should be absolutely flat. So, if you are laying over old floorboards you may have to cover them first with hardboard to provide a suitable surface, especially for lino which is susceptible to cracking and may crack along ridges formed over the floorboards. Do this by nailing the hardboard into the underlying floorboards. You should only lay on concrete if it has a damp-proof membrane (DMP).

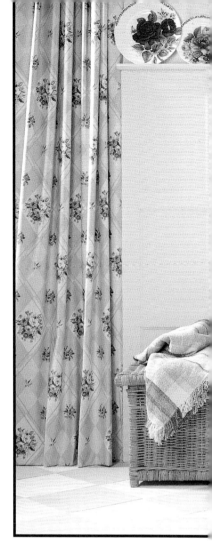

Tiles

Tape measure

String

Chalk

Notched spreader

Tile adhesive

DIY knife

## WHAT TO DO

**1** Calculate the number of tiles you need by measuring the area of the room (multiply the length by the width). Then work out how many tiles fit into 1 sq m (yd) and multiply this by the number of sq m (yds) required. Allow extra tiles (about 5 per cent) for breakages and mistakes.

**2** If laying cork or vinyl tiles they need to be unwrapped and left in the room in which they are going to be laid for 24 hours.

**3** Measure the centre point of the room by finding the centre of the two end walls. Mark the centre points and then using a piece of string which

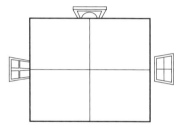

you have rubbed with chalk, stretch the string between the two marked points. Next find the centre points of the other two walls and mark with chalked string in the same way. Snap the string against the floor and the floor will be marked out into four sections.

**4** Dry lay a line of tiles from the centre outwards. The space left between the wall and the final tile should not be less than half a tile. If it is, adjust from the centre to avoid small gaps.

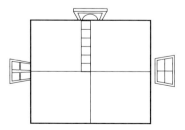

**5** Starting from the centre, use a notched spreader to apply the tile adhesive over about 1 sq m (yd) of the floor. Lay the first tile at the point where the chalk lines cross. Butt the next tile up against this tile and so on, working outwards towards the wall in the order shown.

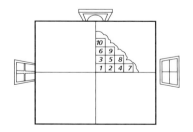

*Left* This combination of lemon yellow and blue-grey tiles laid in a traditional chequerboard pattern gives a young, contemporary feel. Vinyl tiles such as this are relatively easy to lay yourself. Experiment with different patterns or try creating a border design around the edge before sticking them down.

6 To fit the edge tiles, take the tile to be laid and place it over the last complete tile. Take a spare tile and place it over the tile where the last cut tile ends. Mark the line of the overlap on the tile to be cut, remove the spare tile and cut accordingly with the DIY knife. Fix the tile in place in the same way as the rest.

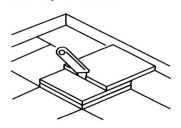

7 Cut corners in the same way. First butt up the tile to be cut against one wall, and then align the spare tile as before. Then, without turning the tile to be cut, turn the spare tile to align with the other edge.

8 To cut around doorways and architraves, you will

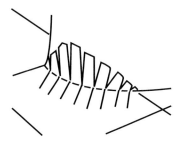

need to make a template from thin card to get the exact shape or you can buy a special template former.

# Laying hard tiles

Just as with soft tiles, it is essential when laying hard tiles that the sub-floor is level and damp proof. If you are laying over floorboards then they should be covered with chipboard or plywood first. Ceramic tiles should be laid on a layer of ceramic tile adhesive (a make recommended by the manufacturer) while quarry and terracotta tiles should be laid on a bed of mortar. Hard tiles are difficult to cut so use a special tile-cutting machine.

## WHAT TO DO

### YOU WILL NEED

You will need

Tiles

Tape measure

String

Chalk

Notched spreader

Tile adhesive/mortar

Spacers

Tile cutter

Tiling grout

**1** Calculate the number of tiles you need by following step 1 of Laying soft tiles on page 46 and then find the centre of the room by following steps 3 and 4.

**2** Start from the centre outwards. If you are laying ceramic tiles use a notched spreader to apply the adhesive over the sub-floor, covering about 1 sq m (yd) at a time.

**3** Press down the tiles using spacers in between to keep them separate to allow for the grouting. You can buy plastic spacers or improvise with small pieces of wood. If you are laying quarry tiles then press them down into the mortar, again using spacers to keep them separate.

**4** Use a tile cutter to cut the tiles to the correct fit for around the edge of the room (see steps 6 and 7 on page 47).

**5** When the adhesive or mortar has dried, remove the spacers and apply the grout with a plastic spreader. Wipe off the excess grout with a damp cloth before it sets.

**Above** These floor tiles reproduce exactly the classic look of the halls and porches found in many Edwardian period buildings.

**Right** These beautifully patterned and coloured Provençal tiles need no further embellishments in a room. Keep wall coverings and furnishings simple so they can be enjoyed.

# Care and maintenance

❖ Ceramic tiles: sweep and damp-mop with a detergent solution. Do not polish the tiles as they will become slippery.

❖ Quarry tiles: once laid, these should be sealed with a mixture of 1 part linseed oil to 4 parts turps - used sparingly. Clean off any white patches by wiping with a mixture of 15ml (1 tbsp) of vinegar and 560ml (1 pint) of water.

❖ Marble tiles: never use harsh abrasives on marble as they will scratch the surface. Damp-mop and rinse with fresh water. Use a silicone wax to bring out the shine, or a special polish. Marble stains quite easily, especially if the substance is acidic, so if you are planning to lay a marble floor in your kitchen take care if you are making black-currant jam.

❖ Slate tiles: these should be washed with a solution of washing soda and water. For a lustrous shine, wipe over with a little milk.

❖ Stone slabs: sweep and wash. Cover oil and grease stains with sawdust, leave and then brush off.

❖ Cork tiles: sweep and wash lightly to keep clean. Occasionally they may benefit from another layer of sealer if they aren't the pre-sealed variety, although even the latter may benefit from a coat of sealer when first laid to prevent liquids seeping between the joints. Try to avoid using spirit-based chemical cleaners.

❖ Lino: this should be swept or vacuumed to remove dust, then damp-mopped with a detergent solution. Do not seal the surface, but use a water- or solvent-based polish to give a soft sheen. To shift scuff marks, rub gently with a pad of very fine steel wool.

❖ Vinyl: vacuum this surface to remove grit which scratches the surface. Damp-mop with detergent solution but don't over-wet tiles as water may seep underneath.

# SHEET FLOORING

Vinyl, lino and rubber are all available in sheet form as well as tiles. The beauty of the sheet version is that if you have a large surface area to cover it is so quick to lay - much quicker than laying floor tiles. Also, as it is now available in 3 and 4m (9 and 12ft) widths you can get an almost seamless finish in most rooms. It is particularly good for laying around non-uniform areas such as a curved alcove or kitchen breakfast bar. Practical and durable, it can be laid in any room and because it comes in such a range of patterns and styles you can find something to emulate almost any other flooring whether it be slate, marble or quarry tile, a sponged or colourwashed paint effect, wood or stone.

It is particularly good in kitchens, bathrooms and children's bedrooms where you want a flooring that is soft and warm underfoot but is waterproof, can be cleaned easily and is safe. The only drawback of sheet flooring is that the rolls can be unwieldy to handle. Lino can be quite brittle too and laying is best left to a professional as it can crack quite easily while still soft. If you do wish to attempt to lay it yourself, read the manufacturer's instructions carefully.

Whatever type of sheet flooring you choose (see Tiles What's what, page 44), the same requirements are needed of the sub-floor as for laying tiles. It should be dry, clean and smooth. Also, do not lay vinyl over timber floors treated with preservative, brown asphalt tiles or asphalt floors, cork tiles or linoleum. Ask your supplier for details of a barrier material to lay between the floor and the vinyl.

**Right** *Sheet lino provides a clean and practical covering for a kitchen floor and comes in a great variety of colours and patterns. This pastel yellow lino with grey border provides an original look which blends well with the rest of the interior.*

**CHOOSING WHAT YOU NEED:**

What's what (see pages 44-5)

**USING SHEET FLOORING:**

Laying sheet flooring

Care and maintenance

# USING SHEET FLOORING

## Laying sheet flooring

Lino should be left to acclimatize in the room in which it is to be laid for about 24 hours, and in very cold weather vinyl needs to be warmed before laying. To ensure a good fit, make a floor pattern first. This is particularly useful in areas such as bathrooms where there are lots of irregular shapes to cut around. Do this with paper underlay and get enough to cover the floor twice.

**Right** This tile-effect sheet vinyl could be used in any number of rooms but here it works well in a hallway. Hard wearing and easy to clean, it is possible to lay sheet flooring yourself although the rolls can be rather unwieldy.

## WHAT TO DO

**1** Lay out your vinyl upside down on a clear, level space in another room (this method can also be used for carpets). Clear the bathroom floor, remove any tacks and make sure the surface is clean and flat.

**2** Cut off enough paper underlay to cover the largest areas of the floor. Then add more piece to fit around the edges, sticking them down to your main piece with masking tape and cutting carefully round all plinths, pipes and bases.

*Below Some vinyl imitates the original so closely that it is hard to tell the difference between it and the real thing as can be seen from this cork-effect flooring.*

**3** Where the paper completely surrounds a pipe or plinth, cut a straight line from the fitting back to the wall in the least visible place, so that the paper can be picked up in one piece.

**4** Lay the template on to your floor covering - again upside down - and tape it down flat so that it cannot move. Trace around it with a fine felt-tip pen, allowing a 7.5cm (3in) trim allowance and marking access cuts. Then carefully remove the paper.

**5** Cut out the shape with the DIY knife as carefully as possible. Lay the grey paper back on the floor to use as an underlay, then lay your new flooring over the top and trim to fit. You should have an absolutely perfect result.

## Care and maintenance

❖ Both lino and vinyl need to be swept or vacuumed regularly to remove dust and grit and damp-mopped with a detergent solution (see also page 49).

❖ Do not seal the surface, but use a water- or solvent-based polish to give a soft sheen.

❖ To shift scuff marks, rub gently with a pad of very fine steel wool.

❖ Make sure that you lift heavy pieces of furniture over both vinyl and linoleum otherwise it may rip and pull up the surface.

### BRIGHT IDEAS

❖ Using offcuts from different coloured pieces of vinyl, cut out shapes from the main vinyl and use them as templates to make replacements from the contrasting colours. These could be triangles, or something more ambitious like a Matisse silhouetted figure for a kitchen, or teddy bears for a child's room.

❖ If you have leftover pieces of lino, older children may like to use them to make lino cuts.

# WOODEN FLOORING

Old or new, the smooth textures of natural wood floors are the perfect solution for practically any decorating scheme whether it is to bring a traditional country look to a period setting or a mellow warmth to a contemporary one. Softer underfoot than quarry or terracotta tiles but equally hard-wearing, wooden floors can be used throughout the house. In a living room or bedroom, a wooden floor can be jazzed up with rugs and kelims for added warmth and colour, while in the hallway a plain wooden floor makes a stylish impression, is hard-wearing and easy to clean.

Old wooden floorboards sanded down and sealed or stained give a rich glowing warmth (see pages 60-3) or if they are not in good enough condition then painted floorboards can work equally well. Alternatively, if you don't have an existing wood floor then there is a huge variety of new wooden flooring to choose from ranging from dark oak to palest ash.

**Right** When stained and sanded, new strip flooring can soon look as if it has been laid for years. The warm tones of this oak finish flooring set against the pale pinks of the plaster walls provide a harmonious combination that is just right for this rustic hallway.

CHOOSING WHAT
YOU NEED:

Hardwood versus
softwood

What's what

**USING WOODEN
FLOORING:**

Sanding a floor

Sealing and varnishing

Care and maintenance

# CHOOSING WOODEN FLOORING

There are two main choices when it comes to wooden floors: you can either strip down an existing floor, or lay new timber flooring over the existing boards or floor. The beauty of sanding down an existing wood floor is that its inbuilt irregularities give it an authentic charm - but remember that good preparation and careful sanding are the key to success (see pages 60-1).

If you have to go for new boards, the first task is to assess the underlying sub-floor. Whatever type of new wooden flooring you decide to choose (see overleaf) it has to be laid on an even, damp-free, and level sub-floor - this means a concrete, hardboard or existing timber floor. Getting this surface right really is essential, even if it means laying down a sub-floor.

## HARDWOOD VERSUS SOFTWOOD

Hardwoods come from deciduous, broad-leafed trees and are generally more expensive and of better quality than softwoods. The range of colours and grains is more varied and includes oaks, mahoganies and birches. Over recent years, the destruction of the tropical rainforests where many of the traditional hardwoods come from has caused great concern. Most suppliers now buy new timber only from managed, sustainable forests with replanting programmes but hardwoods from questionable sources still get through. For the best information, contact Friends of the Earth.

Softwoods come from narrow-leafed evergreen trees such as pine and spruce, mainly from northern temperate regions. The wood is less hard-wearing and stains more easily, but it is cheaper than hardwoods.

**Above** Whether your tastes veer towards the classical or ethnic, a wooden floor will provide the perfect backdrop. Part of the charm of old hardwood floorboards, such as these oak ones, is their irregularity - knots and textures which are full of character and charm.

## PRACTICAL POINTERS

❖ If you are laying a new wooden floor you must make sure that the timber you buy is of good quality and has been properly dried. A good way of ensuring this is to ask whether it has been kiln dried, if it hasn't it may shrink after installation.

❖ Ask an expert fitter to gauge the condition of your existing floor before laying a new one as it is essential that the sub-floor is not damp.

❖ Whether you have a sus-pended or solid floor, all types of wood flooring must be laid on a level, dry sub-floor. If you are laying on concrete it will have to have a damp-proof membrane, and if it is uneven it will have to be overlaid with a self-levelling screed.

**Above** Wood block flooring can come in a number of different patterns such as herringbone, basket-weave and brick.

**Right** Available in different widths and colours, strip flooring provides a practical and attractive surface as can be seen from this living-cum-work area.

# MAKING YOUR CHOICE

You may find that you have old wood floors in your house already such as those described below in Raised wooden plank floors and Solid hardwood floors. But if not, you may choose to install some to your own taste. The descriptions below will help you to make a more informed decision.

## WHAT'S WHAT

**Raised wooden plank floors** These consist of floorboards suspended on joists. If you are lucky you will have hardwood oak floorboards, but many old floorboards are made from softwood such as pine which can be very thin and splinter easily.

**Solid hardwood floors** Wooden floors like this are parquet, wood strips, tiles or blocks that have been laid over a solid floor such as concrete. Finding a solid parquet floor buried beneath your carpet or vinyl tiles is good news indeed.

**New floorboards** If your existing floorboards are in a bad state of repair but you wish to replace them with a similar style of flooring then new boards are your best option. Choose the type of timber carefully, remembering that softwoods such as pine, stain and mark much more easily than hardwoods such as oak.

However, the latter are far more expensive so you could use pine and stain the boards to recreate the look of oak (or the wood of your choice).

Floorboards come in a variety of thicknesses and widths. Obviously the thicker they are, the better the quality. Wide floorboards give a traditional old look to a floor, while narrower width boards are more modern.

**Strip flooring** This is either sold as individual lengths rather like floorboards or in sheets which consist of a number of strips joined together to look like floorboards. The individual planks are tongued and grooved so that they fit

*Below* An immaculately laid new strip floor gives a clean elegance to this interior. It is now possible to buy pre-finished flooring which requires no sanding or sealing.

together without any gaps.

The strips can either be nailed into an existing timber floor or the joists below, or laid as a floating floor over a concrete or hardboard floor using adhesive. Strip flooring is generally made from hardwood which means it is more hard wearing than softwood floorboards, less prone to staining and comes in a greater variety of colours. Like floorboards it needs to be sealed and varnished.

## Wood block flooring

Wood block parquet flooring consists of small blocks of wood all the same size tongued and grooved together in a regular pattern - herringbone, basketweave or brick. Wood block flooring should be glued to the sub-floor and then sealed and varnished. It is an expensive form of flooring and laying should be done professionally.

## Mosaic flooring This

is the cheapest form of wooden flooring and consists of small strips of wood attached to a hessian background. Mosaic flooring comes in square panels which are glued to the sub-floor although some come with a self-adhesive backing. Mosaic floor panels are slightly flexible and are therefore easier to lay than most wooden floors and can

cope with a slightly uneven sub-floor. They will probably need sanding and sealing once laid.

## Pre-finished flooring

This type of flooring is becoming increasingly popular as no sanding or sealing is required. The edges are tongued and grooved and can be fitted together over any level sub-floor. It comes

in strip or in wood block form. The best quality is solid wood while other types consist of a thin layer of hardwood glued to a softwood base.

*Below* This solid oak parquet floor with its traditional herringbone design is extremely hard wearing and if it begins to look scratched it can always be sanded down again and resealed.

# USING WOODEN FLOORING

## Sanding a floor

### WHAT TO DO

**1** Sanding a floor is a very dusty job, so to prevent the dust spreading throughout the house, fix masking tape around the door frame and block the gap underneath the door with newspaper.

**2** Wrap some coarse abrasive paper tightly around the drum of the industrial sander and hold in place with the screw-down bar. Make sure it is secure otherwise it will be ripped off when sanding begins. Put your face mask and ear plugs on - this a really messy and noisy business.

**3** Before switching on the sander, tilt it backwards to lift the drum off the floor. Switch on and lower the machine gently. Begin sanding diagonally from one corner of

the room to the other. Trail the lead behind you over one shoulder. At the far wall tilt the sander towards you, so the drum breaks contact with the floor and turn the machine around. Work your way back across the room on a line just overlapping the first cut.

**4** When you have sanded the whole floor in this way, sweep up the dust and fix some medium abrasive paper to the sander. Sand diagonally across the floorboards again in the opposite direction.

**5** Finally, fix a sheet of fine paper to the drum and sand parallel to the length of the boards to give the floor a smooth finish. Never sand at right-angles to the boards.

**6** You will be left with a strip of unsanded floor all the way around the edge that

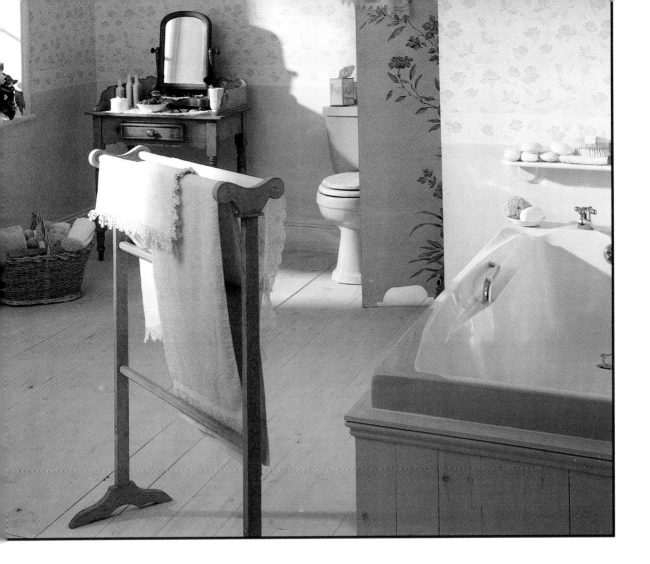

*Above* Sanding down floorboards is relatively easy as long as you have the correct tools. The results can be stunning as can be seen from the bathroom floor shown here. These boards have been sanded and then limed, rather than varnished, to give a natural look.

the drum sander won't be able to reach. Use the hand-held rotary sander here. Again, begin with a coarse-grained paper and work through to a fine one.

7 Sweep, then vacuum the floor and wipe clean with a cloth dampened with white spirit. It is now ready to varnish (see overleaf).

Before you begin sanding a floor it is worth spending time in preparation.

❖ Remove any carpet tacks or nails that are protruding above the boards, or hammer them below floor level with a nail punch.

❖ Fix down any loose boards firmly using woodscrews. The heads of the screws must be driven below the floor surface and hidden under a dab of wood filler.

❖ Fill any gaps between boards with papier-mâché made from newspaper and wallpaper paste and a little water-based wood dye to match the colour of the boards. Fill any large gaps with strips of wood.

❖ Replace any rotten or damaged floorboards. Try to match the new floorboards to the old as far as possible for width, colour, etc.

# Sealing and varnishing

Unless you buy a pre-finished floor, all types of wood floor-ing will need sealing and varnishing to protect them from wear and tear. There are many types of finish available and the type you choose will be dependent on the look you wish to create and the type of flooring used.

Softwood floors in particular need protection and would probably benefit from a wood stain to make them a darker, richer wood colour than their natural pale hue. There are now many different types of stain available ranging from natural wood colours to blues, yellows and reds. Wood stain can also very successfully be used to stencil patterns on a floor.

Undoubtedly one of the best types of finish for a wood floor is a shellac and wax sealer but this is hard to apply and needs re-coating with wax regularly. Oleo-resin sealer gives a tougher finish and retains the character of the wood but needs regular polishing. Probably the most practical and popular finishes therefore are acrylic and polyurethane var-nishes. Hard wearing, resistant to heat and light they are suitable for all floors. You need to apply three coats for a really effective finish.

## YOU WILL NEED

Varnish or wood stain

Large paintbrush

Steel wool

## WHAT TO DO

**1** Before beginning to var-nish or stain the floor, ensure it is clean and dust free and that the room is well venti-lated.

**2** Start in a far corner and work your way back towards the door.

**3** Apply four or five coats in an area of heavy traffic such as hallways and kitchens, three coats in areas that will have rugs or carpets. Allow the varnish or stain to dry between each coat.

**4** Before the final coat, rub over the floor lightly with steel wool.

## BRIGHT IDEAS

❖ Paint a chequerboard design using different coloured woodstains (see page 68). Also see page 68 for dividing the floor into squares and applying masking tape.

# Care and maintenance

Wooden floors are easy to keep clean and if the floor has been well-sealed there should be no problem with staining.

❖ Vacuum or sweep up dirt and use a mop to clean up spillages. Remember, though, that a wooden floor's worst enemy is damp so never over-wet a wooden floor.

❖ If you have laid a wooden floor in the hallway make sure you have a good door-mat as grit and wet can wear away the finish.

❖ If the floor does start to suffer wear and tear, a light sanding and a coat of varnish or wax will quickly rectify the problem.

*Left* A well-sealed wooden floor needs very little maintenance, particulary if you use a polyurethane or acrylic varnish.

# DECORATIVE EFFECTS

If you can't afford expensive floorings, decorative paint effects are one of the quickest and cheapest ways of giving a floor a face lift. If you have cleaned and sanded your floorboards but they're not in good enough condition just to seal, or if you have covered your floor with hardboard or are wondering what to do with your concrete sub-floor, then painting may be your answer.

You can use bright primary colours for a contemporary effect or stencil the floors for an authentic period look. A black and white chequerboard effect could give a room a stark sophistication, for example, while a beautifully marbled floor could give a classic feel. There are endless possibilities and if the worst comes to the worst you can always paint over any mistakes and start again. What's more, it gives you the freedom to be truly creative and to have some fun at the same time. So, why not paint a simple trompe l'oeil rug on a bare floor, or fish on a bathroom floor, or nursery-rhyme characters on the floor of a child's room?

**Right** *Used imaginatively, painted floors can create a stylish focal point to a room for very little cost. This dramatic green and yellow chequerboard floor is simple to recreate (see pages 68-9) and looks stunning.*

# CHOOSING DECORATIVE EFFECTS

There are a number of different approaches you could take to decorating a floor. The wonderful thing about painting a floor is that it can be as simple or as complicated as you wish - both can be equally effective.

## WHAT'S WHAT

**Liming** If you are fortunate enough to have good quality floorboards then you could either sand them down and varnish them (see pages 60-3) or you could lime or wax them, which creates a much paler bleached effect. This latter method was commonly used during the eighteenth century, so if you want an authentic look it is well worth trying out. The floors need to be sanded down first and then liming paste or wax rubbed in with steel wool. It should be left to dry for about half an hour and then buffed up with a duster. The only drawback with this approach is that the floorboards have to be polished with wax frequently; they cannot just be wet mopped as with a varnished floor.

*Right Here a simple freehand design has been painted on to the floorboards which echoes the stencilling on the chest of drawers. If you feel unsure about attempting freehand painting then a simple stencil could be used to create an equally attractive effect.*

**Paint** Perhaps the simplest method of all is to simply paint your floor (making sure it has been correctly prepared) with matt or special floor paint and then apply several layers of varnish to prevent it from wear and tear. You can now buy a water-based varnish which dries much more quickly than the more traditional oil-based varnish and also does not discolour. If your floor is in good condition then you don't even have to sand it down first, just make sure you give it a really good scrub to clean it.

**Above** *Limewashed floorboards have here been decorated with a simple geometric design that picks out the pale pinks of the wallpaper design. To achieve such an effect you would have to draw a floor plan and mark out the squares on the floor to give an accurate finish.*

You therefore have to be sure that the colours and consistency of the paints are correct. Sponging is one of the simplest of paint effect techniques for a beginner while woodgraining and marbling are slightly more complicated.

***Stencilling*** This is a relatively simple technique to use and one that gives instant charm whatever the setting. It looks particularly good over natural floorboards and can be used effectively around stairways and stairwells.

***Woodstaining*** There are now a number of different coloured woodstains available that can give a delicate tint to the floor while allowing the natural grain of the wood to show through.

***Paint effects*** If you want a more decorative surface, however, there are an enormous number of paint effects that can be used effectively on floors such as sponging, woodgraining, marbling and colourwashing. Such paint effects do need a bit of practice as they rely on the application of a top coat of paint over a base coat that shows through.

# USING DECORATIVE EFFECTS

## Painting a floor

Before you begin to decorate your floor, test the colours you wish to use by painting a small area on the surface to be painted and leave them in the room for a while. In this way you can see how different lights affect them and whether or not you like the combination. Varnish also affects the strength of the finished colour (generally making it darker and stronger), so, if possible, try to test this too.

If you are using a light/dark colour scheme you can speed things up by painting the light colour all over the floor before marking out your patterns. It may need two coats for a really good finish. With colours of equal strength, mark out the pattern on the primer basecoat (see below).

### MAKING A FLOOR PLAN

Whatever approach you are going to take, it is essential to make a floor plan before you attempt to decorate the floor. Do this by drawing a scale version of your floor on squared paper and then map out the design you want. It may seem time-consuming but it could save time in the long run.

Allow one square of paper to every 30cm (12in) of your room. Don't worry if your room is not a perfect square as part of the charm of painted floors is that they are not completely perfect. If there are a number of alcoves, however, you may find it helpful to have a plain border around the central floor space to avoid having to account for all the awkward nooks and crannies.

Mark out the central point on your floor plan by following step 3 on page 46. Where they cross is the central point and it is from this point that you should map out the design which, in this case, is a chequerboard pattern made up of 46cm (18in) diamonds.

| YOU WILL NEED |
|---|
| Squared paper |
| Wood primer or concrete sealer |
| String and drawing pins |
| Pencil |
| Large piece of cardboard |
| Ruler and set square |
| Scissors |
| Masking tape |
| Vinyl matt emulsion |
| 4.5cm (1½in) paintbrush |
| Varnish (water-based if possible) |

### BRIGHT IDEAS

❖ If you want a 'hand-painted' look then don't bother with the masking tape and paint around the edges using an artist's brush.

❖ For a busier pattern or a smaller room, use smaller squares.

❖ If you want an aged look, after applying the first coat of varnish wait until it looks suitably distressed, and then add two or three more coats.

## Care and maintenance

❖ A painted floor can be used in any room in the house as long as it is properly sealed. As a rough rule of thumb the more coats of varnish you apply the better it is protected, but you should apply at least two coats.

❖ Varnish wears off in time and to keep it looking immaculate and pristine you will need to apply another coat every two years or so.

## WHAT TO DO

**1** Make sure the surface of the floor is clean. With a roller or large paintbrush, seal the floor with the relevant primer and leave to dry thoroughly. For wood use a wood primer, for concrete a concrete sealer.

**2** Find the centre of the floor by following step 3 on page 46.

**3** Make a 46cm (18in) square template from cardboard using the ruler and set square. Lightly draw over one of the chalk lines from the wall to the centre. Align your template alongside this line and draw the first diagonal of your first diamond.

**4** Using the template mark out the rest of the floor.

**5** Outline alternate squares with masking tape to protect them from the paint. Then using your first colour, paint alternate squares. Leave them to dry and then give a second coat and leave it to dry too.

**6** Remove the masking tape and then apply some more around the painted squares. Paint in the contrasting colours as before.

**7** Touch up any runs or drip marks and when thoroughly dry, sweep the floor and then apply the varnish. Apply at least two coats and allow to dry properly in between layers.

## PRACTICAL POINTERS

❖ The success of a painted floor lies in the preparation as there are many different paints available and depending on the surface you are painting over you will need a different type of primer or undercoat.

❖ If you are painting over concrete, use a concrete sealer.

❖ If you are painting over wood, use a wood primer.

❖ For hardboard, use a wood primer and then undercoat.

❖ If you are painting over wooden floors they may need sanding down first (see pages 60-1) and always make sure that whatever your surface, it is clean and grease free.

❖ If you decide to wax your floor instead of varnishing it, this means it will need frequent polishing and so is probably best confined to areas of the house which are less busy such as bedrooms and dining rooms.

# OUTDOOR FLOORING

In recent years garden 'rooms' have become an increasingly popular aspect of the interior and whether your garden room is a conservatory or a small back garden, or a patio area of a larger space: the flooring you choose has an important impact on the whole scheme.

A natural choice for such areas is one of the hard natural floorings (see pages 44-5) such as granite, slate, marble, limestone and brick. These meet the requirements perfectly as they are hard wearing and pleasing to look at. What could be better for a garden room than a naturally occurring stone, especially if it echoes that used in the interior for a hallway or kitchen? There is no doubt that some of these hard natural coverings make the most beautiful of floorings because of their innate beauty: the individual, stunning patterns of marble, the subtle colour variations of slate or the textural qualities of granite - all have very specific characteristics. They are, however, extremely expensive and if you are looking for a cheaper alternative for your patio or conservatory then you could go for one of the less expensive alternatives such as brick, concrete or – for a driveway - gravel. Brick can look extremely attractive and can be laid in a variety of ways to create different effects - even concrete can be made to look respectable so long as it isn't laid in one unbroken sheet. In slabs of varying shades with plants growing up between the cracks it can look very pretty.

*Right The subtle colour variations and textures of a slate floor make an ideal surface for a conservatory or patio. Here the slate harmonizes perfectly with the blue-greys of the cushions and creates a perfect foil to the rich reds and pinks of the geraniums.*

**CHOOSING WHAT YOU NEED**

What's what

**USING OUTDOOR FLOORING**

Laying a patio

Care and maintenance

# CHOOSING OUTDOOR FLOORING

The properties that make hard floorings an ideal choice for outdoor use are the very same qualities that exclude them from some interiors. They are extremely hard wearing and the fact that they are cold underfoot doesn't matter if they are for outdoor use. Also, because they are natural stone (except for concrete and bricks) they blend in and are sympathetic to an outdoor environment.

If you are lucky enough to already have a natural hard flooring in your house then you may wish to repeat the theme outside to give continuity. If not, and you are planning to have one installed, there are now a huge range of natural materials for you to choose from - you can even buy authentic period stone that has been reclaimed from demolition sites. The main requirement for any type of outdoor flooring is that it should be frost proof: this means that terracotta tiles are generally unsuitable although some types are now given a frost proof glaze.

## WHAT'S WHAT

**Slate** This is a particularly good surface for outdoor use because its natural impermeability means that it does not absorb water. It comes in many different shades from pale blues to deep greys and blacks (see also page 45).

**Granite and limestone** Both these stones are suitable for outdoor (and indoor) use. Granite is an extremely hard rock and comes in a number of different shades of grey and is usually available in large slabs.

Limestone has a warmer, more yellow colour than granite slabs and again comes in large slabs. One of the most popular types of outdoor flooring is York stone which has a wonderful patina.

**Bricks** These are a good value form of outdoor flooring and one that particularly suits town houses. Make sure the bricks you use are suitable for paving and complement the colour and style of your house.

One of the advantages of brick is that it is easier to lay

**Above** *Quarry tiles make the ideal bridge between outdoor room and patio.*

yourself than the above, which are all extremely hard to cut. You can also decide how you want your brick flooring laid as you can lay it to form a herringbone or, brick bond pattern or even like a parquet floor. The bricks should always be laid on a bed of mortar. Because bricks are cheaper and smaller they can also make pretty divisions in ornamental vegetable gardens.

**Cobbles** Traditionally used to pave streets, the look can be emulated for garden paths and patios. It has a rustic, authentic charm and the irregularity suits a cottage garden. Cobbles can be bought from garden centres and should be embedded in clay or mortar. Make sure they are pressed down far enough otherwise they will be impossible to walk on. It's worth remembering that the smaller the cobbles, the kinder they are on the feet.

**Concrete** This is probably the cheapest if, in some ways, the least attractive of options but it is easy to maintain and concrete paving can give a modern and clean look in a contemporary urban environment. Concrete can be laid wet as a continuous sheet or as paving slabs which is easier if you are planning to do it yourself.

**Crazy Paving** This is a generic term that refers to any type of stone set randomly into concrete. It is a good way of using up old and broken tiles and if you have been laying an indoor hard floor and have a small area that needs paving it may be the ideal way of using up any wasted tiles.

## PRACTICAL POINTERS

❖ Smooth surfaces such as concrete are easier to keep clean as dirt tends to collect in the pits and grooves of natural stone.

❖ Gravel is also a practical choice of outdoor flooring and is easy to lay. Its only drawback, however, is that quantities will inevitably end up inside.

❖ Look at magazines or around friends' houses to see what types of outdoor flooring you like. Remember that looking at a slab of granite piled up in a garden centre is very different to seeing it laid flat.

**Left** *The mellow pinky tones of these reclaimed antique pammets are a wonderful, if expensive, choice for an outdoor area. Here they blend perfectly with the stone walls and terracotta pots.*

# USING OUTDOOR FLOORING
## Laying a patio

Whether you are laying slabs of stone, concrete or paving bricks, one of the most important points to remember is that the water must be allowed to drain away from the house. You therefore need to ensure that there is a gradual fall away from the house of approximately 2.5cm (1in) for every 1.2m (4ft) of paving laid. The surface of the patio should also be at least 15cm (6in) below the level of the damp-proof course of the house so that any rain splashing on the paving won't bounce back on to the wall of the house and cause rising damp.

Before digging the site, it is a good idea to lay out the slabs to see how they will fit together.

### BRIGHT IDEAS

❖ Mix different sizes, finishes and colours of slab to create a pattern.

❖ Leave gaps between the slabs so that you can break up the uniformity with small creeping plants.

❖ Use any leftover slabs as stepping stones on the lawn or as crazy paving.

*Right* Stone or concrete slabs make a really good patio surface and are fairly easy to lay yourself.

## YOU WILL NEED

Mortar

Paving slabs

Mallet

Spirit level

Pointing trowel

## WHAT TO DO

**1** Prepare the foundations. Make sure you allow a slope away from the house to ensure any surface water drains away. Starting in a corner (where appropriate), spread a bed of semi-dry mortar over a small area and lower the first slab into position.

**2** Continue adding the mortar and laying the slabs, leaving a 5cm (2in) gap between each. Tap them down gently with the wooden handle of the mallet and use the spirit level to check they are level.

**3** Maintain equal gaps between the slabs using small pieces of hardwood. Work across the top and then down the sides before filling in diagonally.

**4** Continue to check that the surface is level and that the fall away from the house is being maintained. Do this by using a straight-edge and spirit level with a block of wood that has been cut to the gradient of the fall positioned under the bottom of the straight-edge. Tap the slab down or lay it again until you get a level reading.

**5** Fill the joints with a slightly damp mortar mix which can be pressed into place with the pointing trowel. For a good finish, you should mark the joints with the pointing trowel before the mortar sets.

## Care and maintenance

❖ By their very nature, outdoor floorings should need very little maintenance, apart from a good sweep. However, after a damp winter most could do with a bit of cheering up: the main problem will be moss, grass and dirt.

❖ For most surfaces a mild solution of bleach will kill off moss or simply wash down the paving stones with a solution of washing-up liquid and water.

# STOCKISTS AND SUPPLIERS

## Carpets and rugs

**Afia Carpets Ltd**
Chelsea Harbour Design
Centre
Lots Road
London SW10 ORK
0171 351 5858

**Crucial Trading Ltd**
Market Hall
Craven Arms
Shropshire SY7 8ZZ
01588 673666

**The Carpet Bureau**
911 Fulham Road
London SW6 5HU
0171 371 9600

**Interface Europe Ltd**
The Gate House
Gate House Way
Aylesbury
Buckinghamshire HP19
3DL
(for carpet tiles)
01296 393244

**Kayam**
PO Box 319
Wembley
Middlesex HA9 0BR
(Chinese rugs)

**Nice Irma's Ltd**
46 Goodge St
London WIP 1SJ
0171 580 6921

**Tomkinsons Carpets Ltd**
PO Box 11
Duke Place
Kidderminster
Worcestershire DY10 2JR
01562 820006

**Woodward Grosvenor
& Co Ltd**
Stourvale Mills
Green Street
Kidderminster
Worcestershire DY10 1AT
01562 820020

## Cork

**Amorim UK Ltd**
Amorim House
Star Road
Partridge Green
Horsham
West Sussex RH13 8RA
01403 710001

**Siesta Cork Tile Co**
Unit 21
Tait Road
Gloucester Road
Croydon
Surrey CRO 2DP
0181 683 4055

**Westco FLoormaker Ltd**
Penarth Road
Cardiff
South Glamorgan CF1 7YN
01222 233926

## Lino

**Forbo Nairn Ltd**
Woodside Road
Glenrothes
Fife DY7 4AF
01592 759606

## Tiles

**Castelnau Tiles**
175 Church Road
Barnes
London SW13 9HR
0181 741 2452

**Corres Tiles**
219-221 Chiswick High
Road
London W4
0181 994 0215

**Fired Earth Tiles plc**
Twyford Mill
Oxford Road
Adderbury, Banbury
Oxfordshire OX17 3HP
01295 812088

**H & R Johnson Tiles Ltd**
Highgate Tile Works
Brown Hills Road
Tunstall
Stoke-on-Trent
Staffordshire ST6 4JX
01782 575575

**The Merchant Tiler**
Twyford Mill
Oxford Road
Adderbury, Banbury
Oxfordshire OX17 3HP
01295 812088

**Pilkingtons Tiles Ltd**
PO Box 4
Clifton Junction
Manchester
Lancashire M27 2LP
0161 727 1000

**Stonell Ltd**
Unit 1, Bockingfold
Ladham Road
Grondhurst
Kent TN17 1LY

**World's End Tiles**
9 Langton Street
Chelsea
London SW10 OJL
0171 351 0279

## Vinyl

**The Amtico Company Ltd**
18 Hanover Square
London W1R 9DE
0171 629 6258

**Armstrong World Industries Ltd**
Armstrong House
38 Market Square
Uxbridge
Middlesex UB8 1NG
01895 251122

**Forbo Nairn Ltd**
Woodside Road
Glenrothes
Fife KY7 4AF
01592 759666

**Gerslor Ltd**
43 Crawford Street
London
W1H 2AP
0171 723 6601

**James Halstead Ltd**
PO Box 3
Radcliffe New Road
Whitefield
Manchester M25 7NR
0161 766 3781

**Marley Floors Ltd**
Dickley Lane
Lenham
Maidstone
Kent ME17 2DE
01622 858877

## Wood

**Amorim UK Ltd**
Amorim House
Star Road
Partridge Green
Horsham
West Sussex RH13 8RA
01403 710001

**Junckers Ltd**
Wheaton Court
Commercial Centre
Wheaton Road
Witham
Essex CM8 3UJ
01376 517512

**Kahrs (UK) Ltd**
Unit 1
Timberlaine Estate
Quarry Lane
Chichester
West Sussex PO19 2FJ
01243 784417

**Westco Floormaker Ltd**
Penarth Road
Cardiff
South Glamorgan
CF1 7YN
01222 233926

## OTHER USEFUL ADDRESSES

**National Carpet Cleaners Association**
126 New Walk
De Montfort Street
Leicester LE1 7JA
01533 554352

**National Institute of Carpet Fitters**
Wires House
West Park Ring Road
Leeds LS16 6QL
01532 743721
(supplies list of members who abide by code of conduct. A free leaflet on carpet cleaning is also available [please send SAE])

**International Wool Secretariat**
Development Centre
Valley Drive
Ilkley
West Yorkshire
LF29 8PB
01943 601555
(can supply a list of carpet manufacturers in the UK. The Secretariat also give advice on how to keep your carpets in good condition)

# INDEX

The page numbers in *italics* represent illustrations

# ACKNOWLEDGMENTS

The author and publisher would like to thank the following companies and people for their help with supplying photographs for this book:

Front cover: (main) HB/Trevor Richards; HB/Jerry Tubby; Stonell Ltd; Fired Earth.

Back cover : HB/Trevor Richards.

Page 3, Marie-Louise Avery; page 4, HB/Dominic Blackmore; page 5, Fired Earth; page 6, Fired Earth; page 8, Tomkinsons Carpets; page 9, HB/Jerry Tubby; page 10, Tomkinsons Carpets; page 11, HB/Trevor Richards; page 12, Fired Earth; pages 12-13, HB/Spike Powell; page 13, Tomkinsons Carpets; pages 14-15, HB/Trevor Richards; page 16, Tomkinsons Carpets; page 18, Tomkinsons Carpets; page 20, Tomkinsons Carpets; page 22, Charles Barker PR; page 23, HB/Trevor Richards; page 25, Tomkinsons Carpets; page 26, Tomkinsons Carpets; page 29, Fired Earth; page 30, Marie-Louise Avery; page 31, Crucial Trading; page 33, Crucial Trading; page 35, HB/Jerry Tubby; page 36, HB/Derek Lomas & Ian Gibbs/Littlewoods; page 37, Fired Earth; page 38, Fired Earth; page 41, HB/Dennis Stone; page 42, Stonell Ltd; page 43, Delta; page 44, Fired Earth; page 45, HB/Jerry Tubby; pages 46-7, HB/Trevor Richards; pages 48-9, Fired Earth; page 51, HB/Ian Parry; page 52, Beta; page 53, Marley Floors; page 55, HB/Trevor Richards; page 56, HB/Jerry Tubby; page 57, HB/Trevor Richards and Steve Hawkins; page 58, HB/Dominic Blackmore; page 59, HB/Tracey Orme; page 61, HB/William Douglas; pages 62-3, Riggs PR; page 65, HB/Trevor Richards; page 66, HB/Spike Powell; page 67, Laura Ashley; page 69, HB/Trevor Richards; page 71, Stonell Ltd; page 72, Fired Earth; page 73, HB/Simon Brown; page 74, HB/Dominic Blackmore.

The Author and publisher would also like to thank the National Carpet Cleaners' Association for permission to reproduce their Stain Removal Guide.